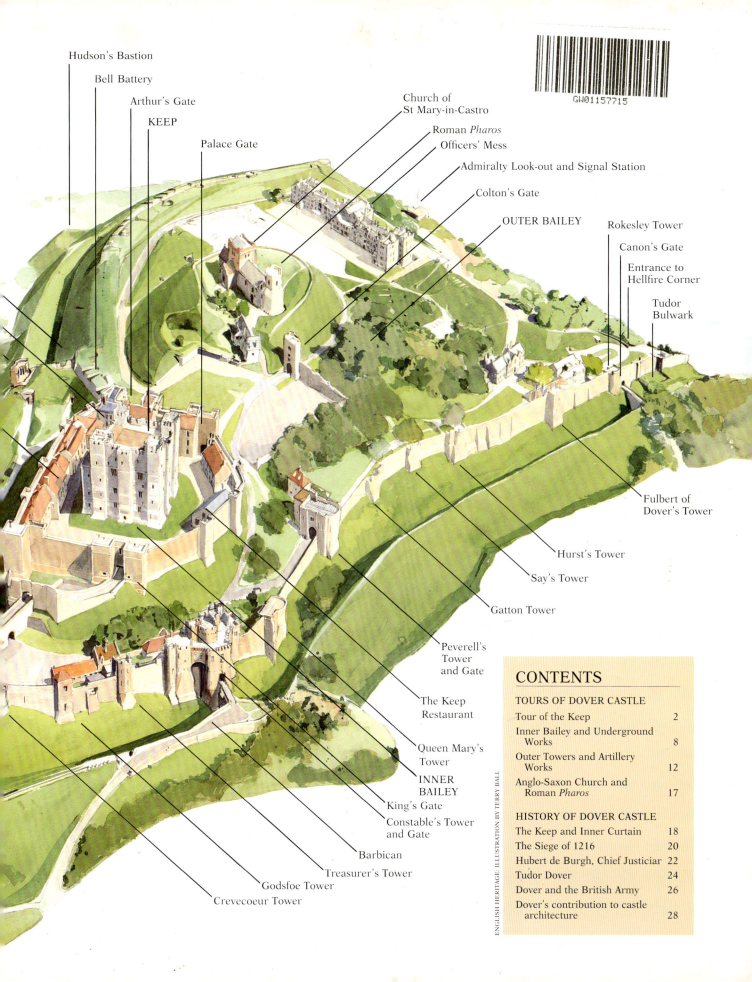

CONTENTS

TOURS OF DOVER CASTLE
Tour of the Keep 2
Inner Bailey and Underground Works 8
Outer Towers and Artillery Works 12
Anglo-Saxon Church and Roman *Pharos* 17

HISTORY OF DOVER CASTLE
The Keep and Inner Curtain 18
The Siege of 1216 20
Hubert de Burgh, Chief Justiciar 22
Tudor Dover 24
Dover and the British Army 26
Dover's contribution to castle architecture 28

Tours of Dover Castle

THE KEEP

Dover's **keep**, or strong tower, was built for Henry II in the 1180s. Round this nucleus, the castle grew. So it makes an obvious start for your tours.

The three-towered **forebuilding**, carrying the keep's entry stairs and the two castle chapels, is one of the most elaborate in the kingdom. A straight flight takes you up into the first-floor **vestibule**, beyond which (immediately in front of you) is a **chapel**. This was the second and the less important of the chapels in Henry's keep, being only half the size of the overlying Upper Chapel, used by the king and his family. Nevertheless, it is richly decorated in the highest contemporary fashion: a mixture of Late Norman (round-headed arches and lavish chevron ornament) and first-period Gothic (delicate attached columns with 'stiff-leaf' capitals and 'water-holding' bases, typical of the style we now call 'Early English' in our churches).

Follow the stairs up, through the arch on the left . They were originally open to the sky so that they could be commanded from the battlements above, and were interrupted by a **drawbridge**, the pit of which still remains. Look back behind you at this point, and you will see the north window of the nave of the private Upper Chapel, over the entry to the first-floor vestibule and again once exposed to the open air.

After the drawbridge, a third flight ascends to the main residential floor of the keep, on the second storey, entered by a

The keep's only first-period entrance was up the steep stairs of the forebuilding

A second flight of stairs, beyond the lower chapel and in the north arm of the forebuilding, was cut by a drawbridge pit, now crossed by a modern walkway. At the top of this flight is the entrance to the royal apartments

These 'stiff-leaf' capitals in the lower chapel of Henry II's keep are clear proof of the modernity of the king's masons in the 1180s, as they experimented with the new Gothic style

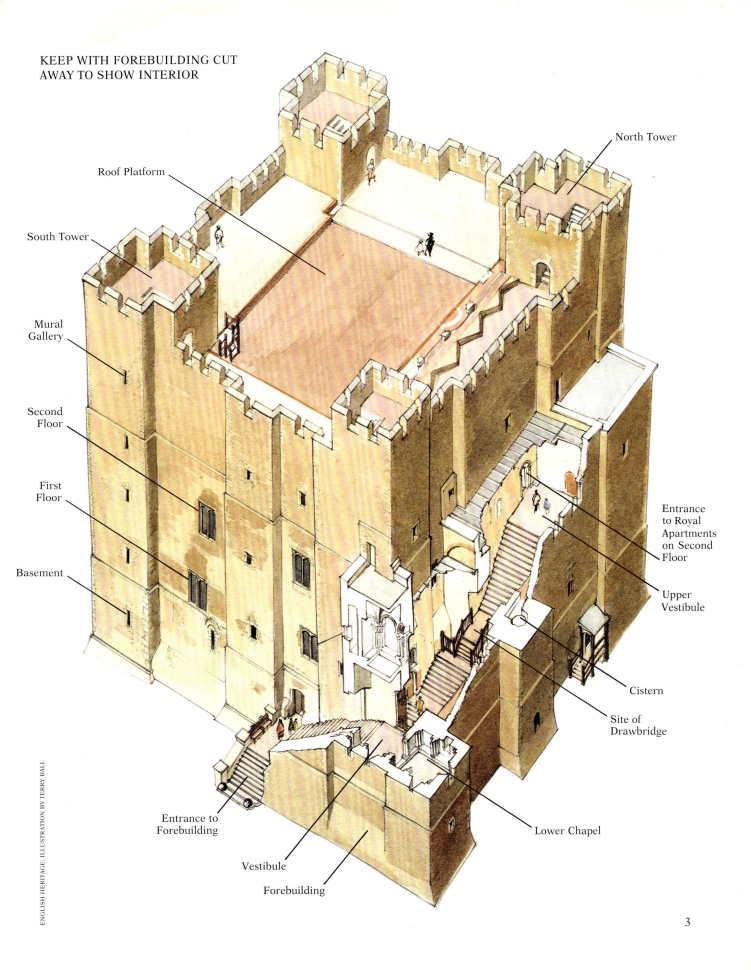

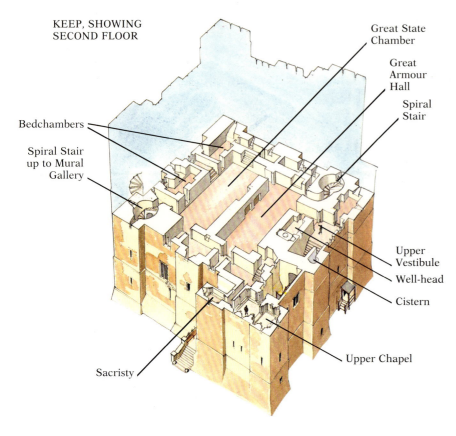

KEEP, SHOWING SECOND FLOOR

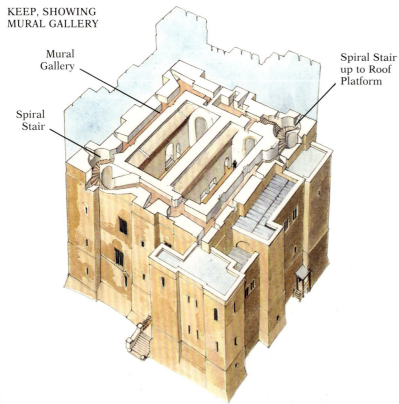

KEEP, SHOWING MURAL GALLERY

grand door (left) in the **upper vestibule**. On the other side of the vestibule, a small chamber contains a circular **cistern**, resembling the top of a well, used for the collection of rainwater from the roof. The real **well-head** is in a vaulted chamber on the left, through the main entrance. Dover's builders brought it to this level for defensive reasons and for the convenience of the castle's most important occupants. Yet water was needed on the lower floors also, and the original lead pipes of the twelfth-century plumbing system can still be seen in a recess to the left.

Much has happened since the 1180s to transform the royal apartments you are now entering. Originally, they rose through two full levels, with upper openings into a surrounding mural gallery. Only one of those openings is still to be seen at the far end of the **Great Armour Hall**; the others have been blocked or are now completely hidden by heavy brick vaults of about 1800, inserted to support guns on the roof. Again at the far (south) end of the hall is the way through to the king's **Upper Chapel**. At the end of a narrow corridor, there is a small **sacristy** to the right, used for the storage of vestments and sacred vessels. On the left, the chapel has both nave and chancel, beautifully proportioned and similar in plan to a parish church. Here Henry II worshipped with his family and immediate entourage. The decorative style, as in the chapel below, is predominantly Late Norman. But Gothic, as there, is also present in many details, most particularly in the pointed arches of the vaults.

Next to the hall, and of equal size, is the **Great State Chamber**, with two smaller **bedchambers** adjoining it to the west. One of these was probably the king's bedchamber. It has a private **lavatory** (garderobe) built into the thickness of the north wall, where it backs on the lavatory of the hall. The fireplace of this chamber, like others in the building, was replaced during the extensive modernisations of Edward IV (1461-83), when the keep's windows were also renewed. But its brickwork conceals an earlier stone flue, and Henry evidently went to bed with a fire in his chamber, as well as with a lavatory *en suite*.

Take the **spiral stair** up, at the corner of the chamber. There are two such stairs in the keep, at opposing angles, both of good quality stonework and large size. Stop at the **mural gallery** before climbing further. This gallery had two purposes. It was a continuous fighting gallery, with firing

ABOVE The Great Armour Hall was Henry II's upper hall and main public apartment. This old photograph shows the armour displayed in 1954; it is now housed at the Tower of London

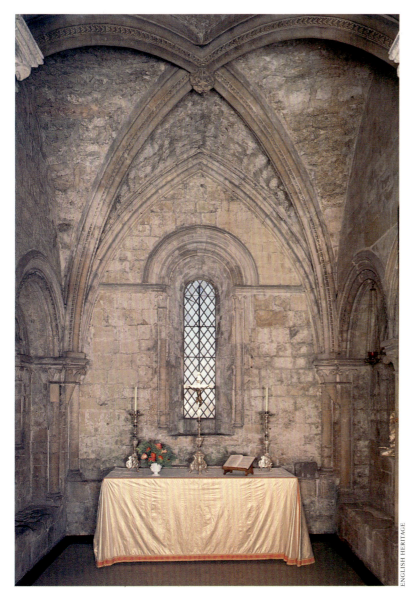

LEFT The King's Chapel was twice the size of the lower chapel. It was richly decorated with wall-arcades and round-headed arches with chevron ornament

BELOW LEFT The lower chapel was splendidly decorated with 'stiff leaf' capitals and chevron-ornamented arches

BELOW RIGHT Spiral stairs in two towers of the keep provided internal access to all floors

KEEP, SHOWING FIRST FLOOR

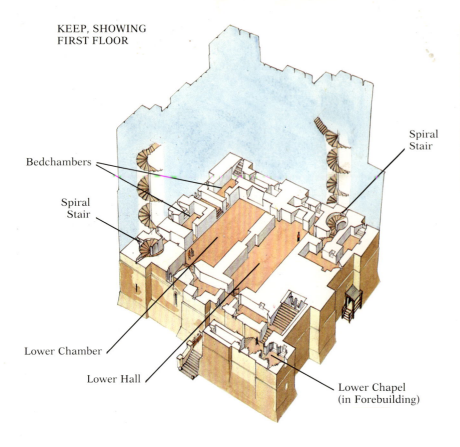

- Bedchambers
- Spiral Stair
- Lower Chamber
- Lower Hall
- Spiral Stair
- Lower Chapel (in Forebuilding)

KEEP, SHOWING BASEMENT

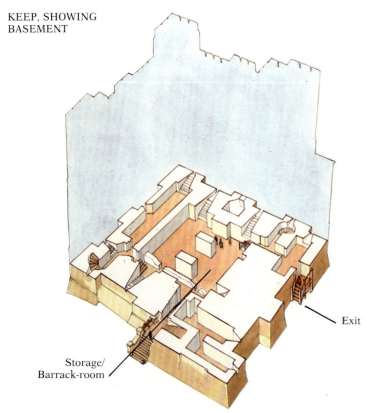

- Exit
- Storage/Barrack-room

The roof platform of the keep, strengthened by Georgian military engineeers to carry guns, is still the best viewpoint for the town below

loops in the outer walls, round which the defenders could move quickly under cover. But it also served to light and ventilate the king's hall and chamber, into which there were once numerous large openings.

Follow the gallery round to the other spiral stair, and continue your climb to the **roof platform**. The panoramas here are the best in Dover. Note how a battery of guns faced Castle Hill, always Dover's most vulnerable quarter. You will catch a glimpse from this quarter of the low-profile earthworks and heavy artillery emplacements of Fort Burgoyne, largely hidden by trees and modern barracks. The fort was built in the 1860s as a final solution to the problem of holding that higher ground.

Now take the spiral stair down to the first floor of the keep, where an exhibition is currently displayed. The plan of the first-floor apartments repeats exactly that of the royal chambers above, with a **lower hall** and a **lower chamber**, and with **bedchambers** similarly equipped. Where the floors differ is in the quality of the window mouldings and in the height of the apartments, only the king's chambers rising through two levels.

At the far end of the lower chamber, in its south-west corner, descend the other spiral stair to the **basement** and **exit**. The basement was at first used only for storage, but may later have been converted into residential use as a third hall, or barrack-room, for the garrison. Across its lower end, a waist-high transverse wall probably carried a timber screen separating off a service passage as was usual in halls of this date.

RIGHT The great keep of Dover Castle, built for King Henry II in the 1180s

Map showing the tour of the Inner Bailey, the King's Gate and Underground Works

THIS PAGE The King's Gate (centre right) with the keep in the background. The entrance to the Underground Works is in the left foreground

INNER BAILEY AND UNDERGROUND WORKS

Now that you have been into the keep, you will probably appreciate better its huge size and the complexity of its entrance arrangements. On the way to Arthur's Hall, look back at the keep's corner (its south east angle), and you will see how the stair-carrying **forebuilding** runs the full length of the great tower's eastern side, wrapping it round also on the south.

Nothing as ambitious as this had been attempted before in English castle-building. Nor was there ever such another to supersede it.

In Dover's earliest days, the castle's inner court (bailey) would have been packed with buildings: living quarters and kitchens, workshops, stores and stables. All these have been replaced or rebuilt so completely as to preserve only the faintest traces of earlier work. The most substantial medieval remains are those of

the great hall, built in 1240 for Henry III and subsequently known as **Arthur's Hall**, recalling the hero of chivalry. The hall, which was incorporated in an eighteenth-century barrack block, has been excavated down to original floor-level. Its best-preserved features are three blocked doors at the lower (or service) end, formerly connecting with the kitchen and other offices. The king's high table, at the other end, backed on the wall now carrying the barrack-room chimney-stack.

ABOVE *At the lower end of Arthur's Hall, built for Henry III in 1240, these three doorways gave access to the service rooms. At Dover, as at other royal residences of the period, there was a growing demand for domestic comfort*

Most of the remaining inner-bailey buildings are of the same date as these **barracks**, built in the 1750s to hold a much enlarged garrison. These interesting early barracks distinguish neatly between officers and men: the former enjoying round-headed windows, the latter having to content themselves with square. At ground level, the **'All the Queen's Men'** exhibition tells the story of the Queen's Regiment, England's senior infantry regiment, having a long association with Dover Castle.

Continue round the court until you reach the **King's Gate**, which took its present form in a remodelling of the mid-nineteenth century. A short way beyond, and down a flight of steps, is the entrance to Dover's **Underground Works**, unique to the castle and not something any visitor should miss.

The works are of two periods. Built initially by Hubert de Burgh after the siege of 1216, they were adapted in 1801-3 by Georgian engineers who were as preoccupied as Hubert with the perpetual problem of deflecting attack from Castle Hill. Broadly, the surviving stonework indicates Hubert's earlier work; the brick is Georgian or later. Where left exposed, the chalk-cut passages are also medieval, as is the circular St John's Tower, in the base of the moat and at its centre.

The attack in 1216 had concentrated on the castle gate, at that time on the outer defensive circuit (curtain) north of King's Gate. Hubert blocked the old gate, and re-sited Dover's entrance to the west, at Constable's Tower, where the slope gave it better protection. However, he was left with the problem of the high ground to the north, against which he opposed a whole new arsenal of defence works. The former gate was converted into the present **Norfolk Towers**, a threatening phalanx of three. Beneath them, a chalk-cut passage ran down into St John's Tower, issuing beyond in the circular outwork which was later re-shaped and cased in brick as the Redan.

Hubert's passage still takes you as far as **St John's Tower**. From there, you can proceed directly into the Georgian **caponier**, a moat-spanning battery on two levels. Descend to the lower level to cross over to the **Redan**, where you will enter an ingenious three-door **vestibule**, still underground, which fed the sally-ports of Hubert's men-at-arms. Take the left of these passages and you are once again in the Napoleonic period. Here a warren of **guardrooms** protects the entrance from the **Spur**. Remote-controlled doors, worked by iron bars from the adjoining chamber, are still in place. Even if an enemy had penetrated thus far, he would have been halted almost at once by a heavy iron-shod door, blocking entirely the cross-moat passage and released from the caponier above.

Guns are still in place in the upper battery of the caponier. At the far end of the entrance, now closed, to the bomb-proof underground passages and guardrooms of the Redan

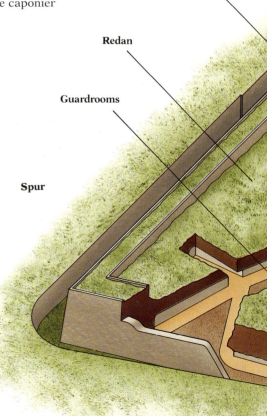

Caponier – battery on two levels

Redan

Guardrooms

Spur

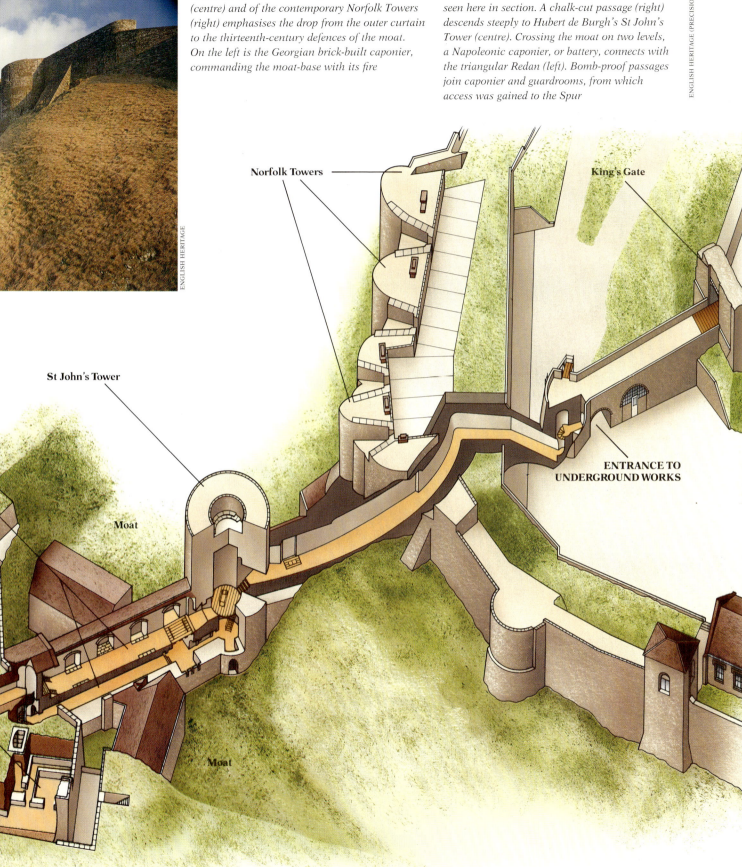

This view of Hubert de Burgh's St John's Tower (centre) and of the contemporary Norfolk Towers (right) emphasises the drop from the outer curtain to the thirteenth-century defences of the moat. On the left is the Georgian brick-built caponier, commanding the moat-base with its fire

BELOW *Dover's unique Underground Works are seen here in section. A chalk-cut passage (right) descends steeply to Hubert de Burgh's St John's Tower (centre). Crossing the moat on two levels, a Napoleonic caponier, or battery, connects with the triangular Redan (left). Bomb-proof passages join caponier and guardrooms, from which access was gained to the Spur*

Map showing the tour of the outer towers and walls

OUTER TOWERS AND ARTILLERY WORKS

The third tour is a long one. You can start it, as here, from the Underground Works; or you can join it (or cut it short) at any point. Much obviously depends on the weather. As you leave the Underground Works, stop to take a look at **Queen Elizabeth's Pocket Pistol** (shown on page 20), housed in the former firestation casemate near the entrance. It is a remarkable cannon, a twelve-pounder 'basilisk' over seven metres in length. Made in Utrecht in 1544, the Pistol was given to Henry VIII by his long-term rival and recent enemy, the Emperor Charles V. Study in particular the lavish Renaissance ornament on the barrel: allegorical figures, vases, and acanthus. New to the North, it was Renaissance engineering, as applied to guns, which rendered Dover's medieval fortifications out of date.

Next follow the path leading up on to the rampart. From the top, you will see (on your left) the mutilated crowns, cut down by Georgian engineers to rampart-level, of Hubert de Burgh's **Norfolk Towers**. Beyond is the re-cut triangular **Spur**, the castle's most ambitious outwork, and within it the brick-built **Redan**, a smaller triangle, which incorporates the bomb-proof guardrooms you have visited. A glimpse can be got of the **caponier** next to St John's Tower, as of another similar eighteenth-century caponier which spanned the moat by the **Fitzwilliam Gate**, on your right. That gate, built in the 1220s by Hubert de Burgh as Dover's postern or secondary entrance, was originally equipped with an elaborate stone barbican and with underground works of its own. It has the twin beak-shaped towers of the most sophisticated French gatehouses, and stood at the summit of contemporary design.

As sophisticated for another purpose was the earlier **Avranches Tower**, at the southern corner of the same curtain wall. You will need to come down from the rampart to reach it, passing nineteenth-century **magazines** (left) and the lofty **towered curtain** (right) of Henry II's inner bailey on the way. Once at Avranches, what you walk through is an upper fighting gallery; stacked above others, and covering the eastern moat with enfilading fire (sweeping its length) through elaborate triple archery-loops. Nothing better was achieved in flanking systems before the artillery bastions of the Tudor Renaissance.

Hubert de Burgh's triple Norfolk Towers (top centre) closed the earlier northern gate undermined in the siege of 1216. In front of them is the circular St John's Tower (centre) and the triangular beak of the Redan. Note the levelling of all towers along this length of the outer curtain to improve the eighteenth-century gunners' field of fire

The polygonal Avranches Traverse at Dover is a purpose-built archery tower dating to the 1180s and at the forefront of contemporary castle design. It has stacked fighting galleries and a bank of triple firing-loops so distributed as to command the entire moat

The Avranches Tower was open-backed to facilitate recapture if overrun. Beyond it (top left) is Horseshoe Bastion one of three massive artillery works on the eastern flank of the castle built in the Napoleonic period

A good place to look back on Avranches Tower is the eastern rampart beyond Bell Battery. But stop at the Battery first, and if your interest ceases with the medieval period, this is where you cut the tour short. **Bell Battery** was built in the 1750s during the Regular Army's first programme of improvements at Dover Castle. It faces the high ground on Castle Hill from which an enemy was most likely to attack. Dover's military engineers returned to the same problem in the Napoleonic Wars, under threat of invasion by the French. It was in this period (1793-1815) that the **east rampart** was raised to strengthen the existing thirteenth-century curtain. On your way south along the rampart, you will pass heavy guns still in place on their sloping recoil platforms, covering the far side of the valley. Below, beyond the moat, are the overgrown earthworks of three contemporary bastions, commanding the lower slopes and valley floor. **Horseshoe Bastion** (east of Bell Battery), **Hudson's Bastion** (at the next angle to the south), and **East Demi Bastion** (at the cliff edge), could all be reached by underground passages from the main rampart. They incorporated batteries, magazines, and quarters for the gunners, each defendable as a fortress on its own.

Bell Battery, originally of six guns, was an early attempt by the Army's engineers to counter the threat from the rising ground on Castle Hill. It dates to the first programme of re-fortification in the 1750s

The Admiralty Lookout Station was well-placed as a viewpoint for Channel shipping, being Dover's latest contribution to modern war

Towards the seaward end of the great east rampart, the views over the Ferryport are outstanding. When you have seen all you want, proceed almost to the cliff edge, which is the best place to study the bleak concrete skeleton of Dover Castle's response to the Kaiser's and Hitler's Wars, the now abandoned **Admiralty Lookout and Signal Station**.

Make your way down to the terrace in front of the huge **Officers' Mess**. It has a vaguely Tudor look and is by Anthony Salvin, a leading architect of the 1850s, whose special interest in the medieval period resulted in much better work in other places. At the west end of Salvin's building, there are further fine views of Dover's modern shipping; especially of the Hoverport below. But look right also at the impressive bulk of the medieval **rampart** which wraps around the church and Roman *pharos*. This steep earthwork has now been dated to the thirteenth century. It incorporates an earlier bank and ditch which could belong to the Conquest period, and may have been part of the castle of the Normans.

Take the steps down from the terrace and you now have a choice. Turn right up the hill towards Peverell's Tower. Alternatively, if your interest is eighteenth-century fortifications, or if you are a keen photographer, continue down the road to **Canon's Gate**, an addition of the 1790s giving better access from the town for supplies and reinforcements to the garrison. Five identical bomb-proof **casemates** (stores and a guardroom) are sited south of the gate, built into the back of the rampart. Through the gate passage, from the bridge beyond, the best view may be obtained of the many-towered outer curtain of the thirteenth-century fortress, with Constable's Gate at the top.

Peverell's Tower, some way up this wall, is where the southern curtain of

The Officers' Mess, a Victorian building, gives fine views of the harbour and town. It was designed by Anthony Salvin who also did restoration work at the Tower of London and built Peckforton Castle

Peverell's Tower is a gatehouse of two periods. On the left is a big mural tower of King John's reign, at what was then the south-west angle of the outer curtain. The semi-circular tower on the right was added in the thirteenth century. Its conical roof probably dates to about 1300

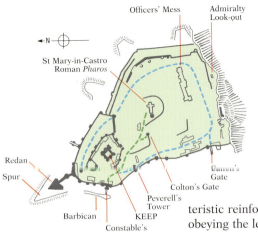

Map showing the tour of the outer towers, the Anglo-Saxon church of St Mary-in-Castro and the Roman lighthouse

Henry III, effectively enclosing a much larger area, meets the pre-siege work of King John. In John's time, Peverell's Tower was only one of a number of big mural towers, although backed in this case by a simple gate. Henry III's engineers added a drawbridge and the semi-circular tower on the right as you approach. It was a characteristic reinforcement of Dover's defences, obeying the lessons of the siege of 1216.

Following the path up now to Constable's Gate, pause for a moment to appreciate the scale of the late twelfth-century **inner curtain**, seen at its most impressive at just this point, with Henry II's keep rising behind. The square towers of the curtain are a diagnostic characteristic of twelfth-century work. From John's time onward, mural towers of this kind were almost invariably semi-circular, reducing the risk of undermining and collapse.

Just such a collapse had been brought about by Prince Louis's miners in 1216. **Constable's Gate**, built in the 1220s to replace the ruined and subsequently sealed north entrance, was Hubert de Burgh's answer to the problem. Across the back of the gate, the Deputy Constable's Lodgings, still in use, are a substantial modernisation of 1882. But the gate passage is medieval, supporting a great edifice which united five towers to make one of the most complex and powerful gatehouses of the period. Where the Deputy Constable now lives Hubert de Burgh had his hall and private chambers. Hubert in person controlled the gate, its portcullis rising into his quarters.

Out on the bridge, look back on the gate. From here, or from the barbican, you can see its forward thrust, facilitating flanking fire along the moat. Even today, overlooked by the walls, the modern approach road climbs a long shallow ramp, incorporating much of Hubert's **barbican**. This is the place to take a final look at the Napoleonic **caponier** to the north, and at its junction with **Redan** and **Spur**. Those dragon-teeth **tankblocks** which march in column up the rampart are the hard-to-credit legacy of a World War II officer who seems to have thought tanks incapable of overturning.

Built in the 1220s as the new castle entrance, Constable's Gate was certainly the greatest gatehouse of its day. Made up of five towers, it projects forwards over the moat, furnishing flanking fire along the walls. Over the gate passage were the quarters of the Constable, Hubert de Burgh – defender of Dover in 1216 and chief architect of the new defensive system

The Roman Pharos and St Mary's Church both pre-date the Norman castle by many years. The lighthouse (left) may be as early as the first century AD. The church is authentic Anglo-Saxon work of about 1000, although much of this was hidden in the 1860s when the building was restored for garrison use

ANGLO-SAXON CHURCH AND ROMAN *PHAROS*

Last of the tours is to the church and former bell-tower, a re-used Roman lighthouse, or *pharos*. Next to the path, **Colton's Gate** is a late-medieval rebuilding of the earlier gatehouse of John's reign, when the fortified enclosure had been much smaller in this quarter. Ramparts link Colton's with Peverell's Gate to the north-west, then circling the church and *pharos* to the east.

If the **Roman lighthouse** has a medieval look, it is because its topmost stage has been rebuilt, like Colton's Gate, in the fifteenth century. Below that stage, the first-century origins of the building are established by characteristic building methods: the use of horizontal bonding courses to level flint-rubble walls, and the alternation of tile and tufa in the arches. There was another similar lighthouse at **Western Heights**, on the opposite headland. It was on those heights, much later, that nineteenth-century artillerymen built a second huge citadel, rivalling the work at Dover Castle itself, and easily made out from its walls.

Next to the *pharos*, the **Anglo-Saxon Church** again looks much later than it is. Disused and roofless in the eighteenth century, St Mary-in-Castro was rebuilt in the 1860s, with aggressive wall mosaics of 1888-89, rightly described as 'quite exceptionally unsympathetic'. Not much of the medieval church survived these improvements. Nevertheless, St Mary's cruciform plan is authentic, and the scale of the church marks it out as a building of former minster status, the home of a community of priests. Notice the exceptionally tall aisleless nave, with high-set windows in each wall; the lofty tower arches and oddly-proportioned south door; and the re-use of Roman tile in many features (faithfully copied by the Victorians). All these are well known in Anglo-Saxon work, dating the building to about the year 1000, two generations before the arrival of Duke William.

A tall rampart (right) circles the Pharos and Church, running north to Colton's Gate (top left), which is a fifteenth-century rebuilding of the original gatehouse of King John

History of Dover Castle

THE KEEP AND INNER CURTAIN

No castle has only one purpose, and Dover's has never been just defence. Henry II's great keep at Dover, both the last and the most ambitious of its kind, has sometimes been seen as an anachronism: out-of-date before even begun. Certainly, it recalls in many details the much earlier tower keeps, among them Rochester and Norwich, built two generations before in the reign of the king's grandfather, Henry I (1100–35). Yet Henry II and his builder, Maurice 'the Engineer', knew very well what they were doing. Henry, who had been brought up in Anjou, spent much of his reign in France: that great laboratory of castle-building in the Middle Ages. Almost twenty years before, for far less money than he would spend at Dover, he had built himself an experimental castle (never repeated in plan) at Orford in Suffolk, which was right up with the latest French fashions. But Dover was a different and greater challenge. The castle was a prestige project, certain to be of high visibility to Henry's enemies. Hubert de Burgh, not many years later, was the first to call Dover 'the key of England'. And so, even as late as the Second World War, it remained.

Henry spent a fortune on Dover: almost an entire year's revenue in total. What resulted was a huge square keep, more sophisticated than it looks, wrapped around by the walls of a multi-towered bailey, similarly characterised by innovation. Brave show was obviously one of the new castle's purposes. Another was the provision of suitable accommodation for the king and for those who rode with him on his travels. Stark though it now seems, there was more than one touch of luxury in

Dover Castle, seen from the north-east, has the characteristically blunted profile of an artillery fortress, very different from the multi-towered look of the great castle of chivalry which, in the twelfth and thirteenth centuries, it had become

ENGLISH HERITAGE

Henry's keep. It was supplied, most exceptionally for a building of that date, with piped water from the well. It was adequately equipped with lavatories, built into the thickness of the walls. There were individual fire places in the royal bedchambers. The keep's two chapels, especially the Upper Chapel which was Henry's own, were finished with appropriate refinement. Two big spiral staircases, at opposing angles of the keep, linked every floor, while another great stair, rising in straight flights through the triple-towered forebuilding, gave direct external access to the second storey.

As advanced as the great tower, and no less monumental, were the defences of Henry II's Inner Bailey. There are no fewer than fourteen regularly spaced flanking towers along the line of the inner curtain at Dover. Henry had used such towers, enabling cross-fire along the walls, at other new castles including Orford. But he had never placed them as systematically as he would at Dover, nor built them on a comparable scale. Pairs of towers, in the north and south walls, protected the gates known as King's Gate and Palace Gate respectively. They are the earliest English gatehouses of that plan.

So much of Dover has been repeated at later castles that it may appear more commonplace than it is. Yet no English tower keep, before Dover's time, had been of equal ambition or complexity. No castle had been equipped with comparable gatehouses, nor with flanking towers of such number or such scale. Even that was not all. In the new outer curtain, planned and begun before Henry's death, Dover anticipated by a century the most sophisticated concentric castles of the later period. It was this outer defensive circuit, extended by King John, which held fast in the siege of 1216.

Henry II, portrayed on his seal, delivers justice to the people

OXFORD: BODLEIAN LIBRARY

The lions of England: the arms of King John

THE SIEGE OF 1216

The Great Charter (Magna Carta) of 1215 was a monument to individual freedom. It has been cited ever since by those in England who have preferred the rule of law over tyranny. Yet in its own time Magna Carta brought peace for just ten weeks. What had been agreed between King John and his barons in June 1215 was already unworkable by August. By October at latest, the nation was in open civil war.

King John, nicknamed 'Softsword', was no general. 'No man may ever trust him', sang Bertrand de Born, 'for his heart is soft and cowardly.' Yet his barons had great difficulty unseating him. Fearing worse things, the rebels offered the English crown to Prince Louis of France, on condition that he came and took it for himself. In May 1216, a French army landed on the south coast.

ABOVE Magna Carta is one of the world's most famous documents. Today it forms a corner-stone of our civil liberties, protecting the individual, through habeas corpus, from the injustice of arrest without trial

RIGHT Windsor Castle was the other royal fortress which, in 1216, Prince Louis besieged along with Dover but failed to take

The fleurs-de-lis of France: the arms of Prince Louis

LEFT *The fury of a siege and its penalties, from a French illustration in the Maciejowski Bible of about 1250. Contemporary armour and weapons typical of the century are shown*

And Louis, before long, controlled much of southern England, including the rebel stronghold of London. Only the royal castles at Windsor and Dover held out.

Both were besieged in late July, but neither fell to the French. Windsor was relieved in mid-September. 'Long were they there', wrote the chronicler, 'and little did they gain'. Dover, invested by Prince Louis himself, was in severe difficulties a month later, but was saved by John's death and a truce. It was at the North Gate — later blocked and rebuilt as the Norfolk Towers — that Louis directed the main thrust of his attack. He first took the gate's outworks, then dug a mine below one of its towers, causing the whole structure to collapse. Hubert de Burgh, defending Dover for King John, blocked the breach temporarily with timber. Nevertheless, the situation had become desperate by mid-October when John, lying at Newark and grievously sick, expired on the wings of a whirlwind.

John's death, during that wild midnight storm on 18 October, was not the end of the civil war he had provoked. For many months yet, the struggle was continued under such picturesque figures as Willikin of the Weald, the royalist guerilla leader, and Eustace the Monk, Louis's admiral. Dover Castle itself, in the spring of 1217, was again under siege by Prince Louis. But its defenders had little to fear. French defeats at Lincoln in May and at sea off Sandwich in August, when Eustace was beheaded on his own ship, compelled Louis and his English allies to accept a settlement. Louis withdrew, but not without honour. Magna Carta was reissued. John, 'nature's enemy', was dead.

The arms of Hubert de Burgh, Constable of Dover and Earl of Kent

A thirteenth-century knight: the effigy of Sir John d'Abernon. A brass from the Church of St Mary in Stoke d'Abernon

THE RECTOR OF STOKE D'ABERNON

HUBERT DE BURGH, CHIEF JUSTICIAR

After King John's siege of Rochester in the autumn of 1215, 'there were few who would put their trust in castles.' Yet he himself put his trust in Dover, and all the siegecraft John had shown in the assault on Rochester was re-applied against his own garrison a year later. At both castles, in particular, the undermining of towers brought about serious collapses. The lesson was not lost on John's heirs.

Hubert de Burgh, Dover's defender, was a veteran who had seen service under the crown since the reign of the late King Richard (d 1199). In 1204, in a rare heroic episode of John's otherwise disastrous Poitou campaign, Hubert had held Chinon for a twelvemonth against the French. As Chief Justiciar of England from 1215, Hubert commissioned castles — Montgomery, Grosmont and Skenfrith among them — which were as advanced as any of their day. Dover benefited also from his skill.

Rochester's loss to its besiegers had begun with a breach in the keep's surrounding curtain. At Dover, it was the outer gatehouse that had very nearly fallen to Prince Louis. Accordingly, Hubert de Burgh's subsequent emphasis at Dover was all on strengthening the castle's outer curtain, without which the keep (as at Rochester) would be a trap. The direction of castle architecture was anyway changing, giving less prominence to the keep. In Hubert's hands, Dover became a castle entirely on the offensive.

Dover's problem had always been the rising ground to the north and north-east of the promontory. To counter this, Hubert blocked the existing north gate, already badly damaged in the siege, and re-sited the castle's entrance towards the slopes on the west, combining it with lodgings for himself. Constable's Gate, still in use, was one of the pioneer residential gatehouses of its era. It was protected externally by a strong defensive outwork. It had a drawbridge, a portcullis, and a long entrance passage. Its towers projected forward over a steep-sided moat to furnish flanking fire along the curtain.

Similarly sophisticated were Hubert's works on the vulnerable northern quarter of the fortress: on the outworks and blocking towers (Norfolk Towers) of the former north gate, and on the new postern (Fitzwilliam Gate) to the north-east. Pointed, beak-shaped profiles characterised Hubert's towers. They were of the latest French fashion, designed to resist undermining. Other measures were taken to prevent an enemy coming too close. Hubert, in his experience whether at Chinon or at Dover, had learnt the value of sorties. To facilitate these, he equipped Dover with its unique system of underground works, each of them issuing in a sally-port. There is a chalk-cut underground passage, beyond the moat, at the far end of the Fitzwilliam Gate barbican. Another passage opens below the drawbridge of Constable's Tower. A third, linking the Norfolk Towers to Hubert's outlying earthwork spur, developed into a whole system of subterranean works, protected in mid-moat by St John's Tower. Any besieging army, after Hubert's day, was more vulnerable than the garrison within. It was exposed to assault at all times and from many different quarters. What it confronted was a fighting machine.

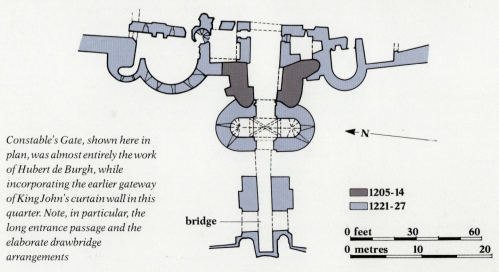

Constable's Gate, shown here in plan, was almost entirely the work of Hubert de Burgh, while incorporating the earlier gateway of King John's curtain wall in this quarter. Note, in particular, the long entrance passage and the elaborate drawbridge arrangements

Hubert de Burgh's purpose in re-siting the main gate was to remove it from the domination of the high ground to the north and to re-establish Dover's entrance on the steep western slope, out of range of contemporary siege engines. Constable's Gate today is much as he left it in the 1220s, though modernised above gate-passage level to provide lodgings for the Deputy Constable

Henry VIII as portrayed in the drawing by Hans Holbein the Younger

TUDOR DOVER

Dover Castle, by the sixteenth century, had ceased to be much regarded as a fortress. Although garrisoned still and kept in fair order, Dover played little part in the fortification programmes of Henry VIII's latter years, when the old king's system of continental checks and balances eventually collapsed at his feet. Threatened by the combined might of the pope's allies — by France and by Spain in rare union — Henry VIII poured every resource of the English crown into the construction of a chain of coastal batteries. Dover, surrounded by such works, was not one of them.

The reason for this was its remote and lofty position. At Dover today there is a fine gun of the period, known incongruously as Queen Elizabeth's Pocket Pistol. It dates to 1544, was made in Utrecht as a gift to Henry VIII, and carries an inscription which reads (in translation): 'Breaker my name of rampart and wall/Over hill and dale I throw my ball'. The Pocket Pistol has a barrel of extreme length. It could throw its ball over a distance (some say) of seven miles. In contrast, contemporary ordnance of more conventional design had to get very much closer to its target.

One consequence was that Henry VIII's new forts were constructed for the most part at sea level, where they could do battle, gun for gun, with hostile shipping. At Dover, there were three Henrician batteries, all of them down by the harbour. And the only known modification of the castle itself was the Tudor Bulwark, a gun platform towards the south-west corner of the outer curtain. Henry preferred to concentrate his energies elsewhere. Just up the coast, on the sea front at Deal, is one of the earliest and most expensive of Henry's forts, built in 1539–40. Deal Castle is typical of its period, geometrically perfect in plan. Six great circles interlock and are meshed like the cogs of a wheel. Five stacked fighting platforms carry a total of 145 gun embrasures. Nothing better illustrates Henry VIII's obsession with artillery, nor his lack of regard for its cost.

The geometrical plan of Deal Castle

BELOW *Henry VIII had a particular interest in artillery. This great bronze basilisk, 7.3m in length, was presented to Henry by the Emperor Charles V*

ABOVE *A sixteenth-century drawing of the keep and inner bailey by John Bereblock. It shows the original pentice linking Arthur's Hall with the keep and, to the right of the keep, the old south barbican*

ABOVE This painting at Hampton Court Palace depicts the embarkation from Dover of Henry VIII and his court for France in 1521. The subsequent meeting was at the invitation of the King of France and was known as the Field of the Cloth of Gold

LEFT Detail from a 1538 picture map of Dover, drawn for the harbour works survey. The castle is shown at top centre, high above the town

In this 1735 engraving, Dover Castle (top right) is shown shortly before its transformation for artillery. Its towers and east curtain (later hidden in the rampart) are still standing at their full height

Henrietta Maria, Charles I's bride, was not much taken by Dover. Her chamberlain wrote: 'The castle is an ancient building constructed after the manner of olden days, in which the queen was ill lodged in poorly furnished apartments, and her retinue treated with very little magnificence considering the importance of the occasion'

DOVER AND THE BRITISH ARMY

At medieval Dover, defence had concentrated on the castle promontory. Modern Dover saw a new shift of emphasis towards the port. Already, in the sixteenth century, some of this re-shaping had begun. Archcliffe Fort (below Western Heights), Black Bulwark (to its east), and Moat's Bulwark (to the east again, below the castle), covered the Tudor harbour between them. Later generations, most particularly from the 1780s, continued and developed these beginnings.

Dover Castle, in the meantime, rose to brief prominence in 1625 as the reception-point for Charles I's new queen, Henrietta Maria of France. To receive her, the ancient keep was redecorated and refurnished. Moulded plaster ceilings with painted cornices were installed in the royal apartments. At the entrance, a fine stone portico — a 'greate Rusticke (rusticated) Dore' — was constructed, ornamented with 'Rusticke pillausters, and sondry mouldinges, and cornishes', probably to a design by the King's Surveyor, Inigo Jones. Yet the queen and her party remained unimpressed. And whether for this reason or another, Dover entered its long sleep from that time forward, reviving only temporarily for the Civil War (1642–49).

It was another invasion threat, not unlike that of 1539–40, which brought Dover back to life in the 1740s. By 1744, France and Spain had once more united against England. There was a Jacobite army, under Marshal Saxe, mustering ominously at Dunkirk. Over the next decade, until 1756, Dover Castle was fully garrisoned, while its troops were kept busy throughout that period on the modernisation of the medieval defences. For the last time, it was the castle itself which received the lion's share of attention.

New barracks (the Keep Yard barracks) were built against the walls of Henry II's Inner Bailey. Then batteries were constructed to command the north-east quarter: six guns at Bell Battery, another four north of the church and *pharos*. It was during this campaign that the systematic mutilation of the medieval fortress first began. Along the north-east curtain, between Fitzwilliam Gate and Avranches Tower to its south, two late twelfth-century flanking towers were demolished to rampart-level. Dover's blunted profile, as we know it today, is entirely the work of artillerymen.

Further demolitions were required by later gunners, under pressure once again of invasion threats during the Revolutionary and Napoleonic Wars (1793-1815). And Dover Castle, before 1805, had lost all but a few of its upstanding towers, cut off short to improve fields of fire. Even the keep had been bomb-proofed with ugly brick vaults and brought into service as a gun platform. In addition, new artillery bastions had been constructed, with their own elaborate underground works — Constable's Bastion

ABOVE *Western Heights, seen here across the town from Dover Castle, was an artillery fortress of great size and vast expense. Begun in the 1780s, it took over seventy years to complete*

LEFT *The Officers' Mess at Western Heights*

LOWER LEFT *A feature of Western Heights was its 140ft vertical shaft, which held three spiral staircases. The shaft and its connecting tunnel enabled troops to be moved into the fortress directly from the town*

to the west; Horseshoe Bastion, Hudson's Bastion and East Demi Bastion, along the still vulnerable eastern flank. Gun-carrying caponiers had been laid across the moats, one of these below Canon's Gate, itself newly cut as a carriage and troop entrance to the Outer Bailey.

These improvements at Dover Castle were expensive. Yet they were far less costly than contemporary activity on the opposing Western Heights, a huge defensive complex begun in the early 1780s. This new artillery citadel, on the other side of the town, complemented rather than superseded the medieval castle. Nevertheless, it opened a fresh chapter in Dover's defence, in which the role of the older fortress became less central. When eventually, after many delays, the works at Western Heights were finished in the 1850s, they were immediately succeeded by other major projects, only few of which touched Dover Castle. Most important of these, remedying an old lack, was the building (from 1860) of Fort Burgoyne, on the high commanding ground to the castle's east. Most ingenious was the great steam-driven revolving turret down on Admiralty Pier, armed with its pair of eighty-ton 16-inch guns. Many of these works can still be inspected from the walls of Henry II's fortress. Their sequence ends today with the Admiralty Lookout and Signal Station (below the castle on the south), last military link in a chain of rare length, from the twelfth century to the Second World War.

The early concentric defences of Henry II's castle at Dover, finished off by John, are clearly seen in this aerial view of the fortress. North from Avranches Tower (bottom right), a long stretch of the outer curtain had been completed before Henry's death. Hubert de Burgh's innovatory residential gatehouse at Constable's Tower (top left) was Dover's second major contribution to castle architecture

DOVER'S CONTRIBUTION TO CASTLE ARCHITECTURE

Dover twice set the pace in medieval castle architecture, before gunnery drove the fortress underground. Both occasions were accompanied by heavy expenditure, most particularly on the outer defences.

The first of these campaigns, initiated by Henry II, included the construction in the 1180s of the great keep. But there was little that was novel in a building of this kind, apart from its size and its luxury. In contrast, the number and regular spacing of the interval towers on Henry's Inner Curtain were virtually unprecedented in his kingdom. Dover's even more ambitious Outer Curtain, begun before Henry's death and continued by his sons, heralded a new era in castle planning.

Concentric defence in this mode, where a high inner wall overlooks and commands its outer ring, took a further full century to perfect. Edward I's North Welsh castle at Beaumaris, begun in 1295, was never bettered afterwards by fortress-builders. In the meantime, however, Dover had established another major first in military engineering. Dover's greater gatehouses were all rebuilt by Hubert de Burgh, following his siege experience in 1216 when the castle had nearly fallen to Prince Louis. The residential gate house (Constable's Tower) and the sophisticated stone barbican (St John's Tower and Fitzwilliam Gate), each set a standard for later imitators. From that time forward, the keep lost much of its priority in defensive systems, to be replaced almost everywhere by the gatehouse. Dover had met and had overcome its last challenge.